Copyright ©2020 LISA H. GREGORY PH.D

All rights reserved. No part of this publication may be reproduced, distributed, or transmitted in any form or by any means, including photocopying, recording, or other electronic or mechanical methods, without the prior written permission of the publisher, except in the case of brief quotations embodied in critical reviews and certain other noncommercial uses permitted by copyright law.

CONTENTS

Introduction
Chapter one
    Bee colonies
    Species
    Castes
    Queen bee (center)
    Mating of queens
    Worker bee
    Period Work activity
    Drones
    Annual cycle of a bee colony
    Formation of new colonies
    Factors that trigger swarming
    Artificial swarming
    Diseases
    Parasites
    Predators
    The Secrets of Beekeeping
        Challenging Times for Beekeepers and Bees
        Safety Gear
        Inside a Beehive
    History

    Scientific study of honey bees
    Invention of the movable comb hive
        Evolution of hive designs
    Fixed comb hives
    Modern beekeeping
    Vertical stackable hives
    Protective clothing
    Smoker
    Effects of stings and of protective measures
    Natural beekeeping
Conclusion

INTRODUCTION

Beekeeping, also apiculture, management of colonies of bees for the production of honey and other hive products and for the pollination of crops. Beekeeping usually refers to the husbandry of the European honey bee, but it may also refer to management of other species of social bees, such as the Indian honey bee, the dwarf honey bee, or stingless bees. Groups of hives are called apiaries, and a beekeeper may also be called an apiarist or apiculturist.

An ancient and widespread profession, beekeeping is believed to have originated in the Middle East. The early Egyptians kept bees and traded for honey and beeswax along the East African coast several thousand years ago. Until 1851, beekeepers harvested honey and beeswax by killing the colonies inhabiting the hives. In that year the American apiarist Lorenzo Lorraine Langstroth discovered the principle of "bee space": Bees leave spaces of about 0.6 cm (about 0.23 in) between wax combs. In artificial hives, if this space is left between adjacent comb frames and between the end frames and the walls of the hive, each comb will remain unattached to neighboring combs. Langstroth's discovery made it possible to remove individual frames from a beehive and to harvest honey and wax without destroying the colony. It also became possible to control disease and to maintain a larger number of colonies.

Beekeepers worldwide earn their living from the sale of the honey and beeswax their hives produce, but the most important contribution of bees to the economy and the environment is their pollination of fruits, vegetables, and pasturage. In some countries, beekeepers are paid for their pollination services.

Beekeeping is becoming an increasingly popular pastime. The health (and taste) benefits of natural honey, the relaxing qualities of caring for your swarm, and the opportunity to undertake this activity in the wonderful outdoors act as a draw for many budding gardeners and country folk.

Beekeeping is a wonderfully rewarding and relaxing pastime. It needn't take up huge amounts of time or cost the earth. Follow this beekeeping for beginners guide and you'll gain an insight into one of nature's most fascinating creatures, not to mention delicious honey.

CHAPTER ONE

BEE COLONIES

SPECIES

There are more than 20,000 species of wild bees. Many species are solitary (e.g., mason bees, leafcutter bees (Megachilidae), carpenter bees and other ground-nesting bees). Many others rear their young in burrows and small colonies (e.g., bumblebees and stingless bees). Some honey bees are wild e.g. the little honeybee (Apis florea), giant honeybee (Apis dorsata) and rock bee (Apis laboriosa). Beekeeping, or apiculture, is concerned with the practical management of the social species of honey bees, which live in large colonies of up to 100,000 individuals. In Europe and America the species universally managed by beekeepers is the Western honey bee (Apis mellifera). This species has several sub-species, such as the Italian bee (Apis mellifera ligustica), European dark bee (Apis mellifera mellifera), and the Carniolan honey bee (Apis mellifera carnica). In the tropics, other species of social bees are managed for honey production, including the Asiatic honey bee (Apis cerana).

CASTES

A colony of bees consists of three castes of bee:

A queen bee, which is normally the only breeding female in the colony;

A large number of female worker bees, typically 30,000–50,000 in number;

A number of male drones, ranging from thousands in a strong hive in spring to very few during dearth or cold season.

QUEEN BEE (CENTER)

The queen is the only sexually mature female in the hive and all of the female worker bees and male drones are her offspring. The queen may live for up to three years or more and may be capable of laying half a million eggs or more in her lifetime. At the peak of the breeding season, late spring to summer, a good queen may be capable of laying 3,000 eggs in one day, more than her own body weight. This would be exceptional however; a prolific queen might peak at 2,000 eggs a day, but a more average queen might lay just 1,500 eggs per day. The queen is raised from a normal worker egg, but is fed a larger amount of royal jelly than a normal worker bee, resulting in a radically different growth and metamorphosis. The queen influences the colony by the production and dissemination of a variety of pheromones or "queen substances". One of these chemicals suppresses the development of ovaries in all the female worker bees in the hive and prevents them from laying eggs.

MATING OF QUEENS

The queen emerges from her cell after 15 days of development and she remains in the hive for 3–7 days before venturing out on a mating flight. Mating flight is otherwise known as "nuptial flight". Her first orientation flight may only last a few seconds, just enough to mark the position of the hive. Subsequent mating flights may last from 5 minutes to 30 minutes, and she may mate with a number of male drones on each flight. Over several matings, possibly a dozen or more, the queen receives and stores enough sperm from a succession of drones to fertilize hundreds of thousands of eggs. If she does not manage to leave the hive to mate—possibly due to bad weather or being trapped in part of the hive—she remains infertile and becomes a drone layer, incapable of producing female worker bees. Worker bees sometimes kill a non-performing queen and produce another. Without a properly performing queen, the hive is doomed.

Mating takes place at some distance from the hive and often several hundred feet in the air; it is thought that this separates the strongest drones from the weaker ones, ensuring that only the fastest and strongest drones get to pass on their genes.

WORKER BEE

Most of the bees in a hive are female worker bees. At the height of summer when activity in the hive is frantic and work goes on non-stop, the life of a worker bee may be as short as 6 weeks; in late autumn, when no brood is being raised and no nectar is being harvested, a young bee may live for 16 weeks, right through the winter.

Over the course of their lives, worker bees' duties are dictated by age. For the first few weeks of their lifespan, they perform basic chores within the hive: cleaning empty brood cells, removing debris and other housekeeping tasks, making wax for building or repairing comb, and feeding larvae. Later, they may ventilate the hive or guard the entrance. Older workers leave the hive daily, weather permitting, to forage for nectar, pollen, water, and propolis.

PERIOD WORK ACTIVITY

Days 1–3 Cleaning cells and incubation

Day 3–6 Feeding older larvae

Day 6–10 Feeding younger larvae

Day 8–16 Receiving nectar and pollen from field bees

Day 12–18 Beeswax making and cell building

Day 14 onwards Entrance guards; nectar, pollen, water and

DRONES

Drones are the largest bees in the hive (except for the queen), at almost twice the size of a worker bee. Note in the picture that they have much larger eyes than the workers have, presumably to better locate the queen during the mating flight. They do not work, do not forage for pollen or nectar, are unable to sting, and have no other known function than to mate with new queens and fertilize them on their mating flights. A bee colony generally starts to raise drones a few weeks before building queen cells so they can supersede a failing queen or prepare for swarming. When queen-raising for the season is over, bees in colder climates drive drones out of the hive to die, biting and tearing their legs and wings.

A domesticated bee colony is normally housed in a rectangular hive body, within which eight to ten parallel frames house the vertical plates of honeycomb that contain the eggs, larvae, pupae and food for the colony. If one were to cut a vertical cross-section through the hive from side to side, the brood nest would appear as a roughly ovoid ball spanning 5–8 frames of comb. The two outside combs at each side of the hive tend to be exclusively used for long-term storage of honey and pollen.

Within the central brood nest, a single frame of comb typically has a central disk of eggs, larvae and sealed brood cells that may extend almost to the edges of the frame. Immediately above the brood patch an arch of pollen-filled cells extends from side to side, and above that again a broader arch of honey-filled cells extends to the frame tops. The pollen is protein-rich food for developing larvae, while honey is also food but largely energy rich rather than protein rich. The nurse bees that care for the developing brood secrete a special food called "royal jelly" after feeding themselves on honey and pollen. The amount of royal jelly fed to a larva determines whether it develops into a worker bee or a queen.

Apart from the honey stored within the central brood frames, the bees store surplus honey in combs above the brood nest. In modern hives the beekeeper places separate boxes, called "supers", above the brood box, in which a series of shallower combs is provided for storage of honey. This enables the beekeeper to remove some of the supers in the late summer, and to extract the surplus honey harvest, without damaging the colony of bees and its brood nest below. If all the honey is taken, including the amount of honey needed to survive winter, the beekeeper must replace these stores by feeding the bees sugar or corn syrup in autumn.

ANNUAL CYCLE OF A BEE COLONY

The development of a bee colony follows an annual cycle of growth that begins in spring with a rapid expansion of the brood nest, as soon as pollen is available for feeding larvae. Some production of brood may begin as early as January, even in a cold winter, but breeding accelerates towards a peak in May (in the northern hemisphere), producing an abundance of harvesting bees synchronized to the main nectar flow in that region. Each race of bees times this build-up slightly differently, depending on how the flora of its original region blooms. Some regions of Europe have two nectar flows: one in late spring and another in late August. Other regions have only a single nectar flow. The skill of the beekeeper lies in predicting when the nectar flow will occur in his area and in trying to ensure that his colonies achieve a maximum population of harvesters at exactly the right time.

The key factor in this is the prevention or skillful management of the swarming impulse. If a colony swarms unexpectedly and the beekeeper does not manage to capture the resulting swarm, he is likely to harvest significantly less honey from that hive, since he has lost half his worker bees at a single stroke. If, however, he can use the swarming impulse to breed a new queen but keep all the bees in the colony together, he maximizes his chances of a good harvest. It takes many years of learning and experience to be able to manage all these aspects successfully, though owing to variable circumstances many beginners often achieve a good honey harvest.

FORMATION OF NEW COLONIES

All colonies are totally dependent on their queen, who is the only egg-layer. However, even the best queens live only a few years and one or two years longevity is the norm. She can choose whether or not to fertilize an egg as she lays it; if she does so, it develops into a female worker bee; if she lays an unfertilized egg it becomes a male drone. She decides which type of egg to lay depending on the size of the open brood cell she encounters on the comb. In a small worker cell, she lays a fertilized egg; if she finds a larger drone cell, she lays an unfertilized drone egg.

All the time that the queen is fertile and laying eggs she produces a variety of pheromones, which control the behavior of the bees in the hive. These are commonly called queen substance, but there are various pheromones with different functions. As the queen ages, she begins to run out of stored sperm, and her pheromones begin to fail.

Inevitably, the queen begins to falter, and the bees decide to replace her by creating a new queen from one of her worker eggs. They may do this because she has been damaged (lost a leg or an antenna), because she has run out of sperm and cannot lay fertilized eggs (has become a "drone laying queen"), or because her pheromones have dwindled to where they cannot control all the bees in the hive. At this juncture, the bees produce one or more queen cells by modifying existing worker cells that contain a normal female egg. They then pursue one of two ways to replace the queen: supersedure, replacing or superseding the queen without swarming, or swarm cell production, dividing the hive into two colonies through swarming.

Supersedure is highly valued as a behavioral trait by beekeepers. A hive that supersedes its old queen does not lose any stock. Instead it creates a new queen and the old one fades away or is killed when the new queen emerges. In these hives, the bees produce just one or two queen cells, characteristically in the center of the face of a broodcomb.

Swarm cell production involves creating many queen cells, typically a dozen or more. These are located around the edges of a broodcomb, often at the sides and the bottom.

Once either process has begun, the old queen leaves the hive with the hatching of the first queen cells. She leaves accompanied by a large number of bees, predominantly young bees (wax-secretors), who form the basis of the new hive. Scouts are sent out from the swarm to find suitable hollow trees or rock crevices. As soon as one is found, the entire swarm moves in. Within a matter of hours, they build new wax brood combs, using honey stores that the young bees have filled themselves with before leaving the old hive. Only young bees can secrete wax from special abdominal segments, and this is why swarms tend to contain more young bees. Often a number of virgin queens accompany the first swarm (the "prime swarm"), and the old queen is replaced as soon as a daughter queen mates and begins laying. Otherwise, she is quickly superseded in the new home.

Different sub-species of Apis mellifera exhibit differing swarming characteristics. In general the more northerly black races are said to swarm less and supersede more, whereas the more southerly yellow and grey varieties are said to swarm more frequently. The truth is complicated because of the prevalence of cross-breeding and hybridization of the sub species.

FACTORS THAT TRIGGER SWARMING

Some beekeepers may monitor their colonies carefully in spring and watch for the appearance of queen cells, which are a dramatic signal that the colony is determined to swarm. swarm attached to a branch

This swarm looks for shelter. A beekeeper may capture it and introduce it into a new hive, helping meet this need. Otherwise, it returns to a feral state, in which case it finds shelter in a hollow tree, excavation, abandoned chimney, or even behind shutters.

A small after-swarm has less chance of survival and may threaten the original hive's survival if the number of individuals left is unsustainable. When a hive swarms despite the beekeeper's preventative efforts, a good management practice is to give the reduced hive a couple frames of open brood with eggs. This helps replenish the hive more quickly and gives a second opportunity to raise a queen if there is a mating failure.

Each race or sub-species of honey bee has its own swarming characteristics. Italian bees are very prolific and inclined to swarm; Northern European black bees have a strong tendency to supersede their old queen without swarming. These differences are the result of differing evolutionary pressures in the regions where each subspecies evolved.

ARTIFICIAL SWARMING

When a colony accidentally loses its queen, it is said to be "queenless". The workers realize that the queen is absent after as little as an hour, as her pheromones fade in the hive. Instinctively, the workers select cells containing eggs aged less than three days and enlarge these cells dramatically to form "emergency queen cells". These appear similar to large peanut-like structures about an inch long that hang from the center or side of the brood combs. The developing larva in a queen cell is fed differently from an ordinary worker-bee; in addition to the normal honey and pollen, she receives a great deal of royal jelly, a special food secreted by young "nurse bees" from the hypopharyngeal gland. This special food dramatically alters the growth and development of the larva so that, after metamorphosis and pupation, it emerges from the cell as a queen bee. The queen is the only bee in a colony which has fully developed ovaries, and she secretes a pheromone which suppresses the normal development of ovaries in all her workers.

Beekeepers use the ability of the bees to produce new queens to increase their colonies in a procedure called splitting a colony. To do this, they remove several brood combs from a healthy hive, taking care to leave the old queen behind. These combs must contain eggs or larvae less than three days old and be covered by young nurse bees, which care for the brood and keep it warm. These brood combs and attendant nurse bees are then placed into a small "nucleus hive" with other combs containing honey and pollen. As soon as the nurse bees find themselves in this new hive and realize they have no queen, they set about constructing emergency queen cells using the eggs or larvae they have in the combs with them.

DISEASES

The common agents of disease that affect adult honey bees include fungi, bacteria, protozoa, viruses, parasites, and poisons. The gross symptoms displayed by affected adult bees are very similar, whatever the cause, making it difficult for the apiarist to ascertain the causes of problems without microscopic identification of microorganisms or chemical analysis of poisons. Since 2006 colony losses from colony collapse disorder have been increasing across the world although the causes of the syndrome are, as yet, unknown. In the US, commercial beekeepers have been increasing the number of hives to deal with higher rates of attrition.

PARASITES

Galleria mellonella and Achroia grisella "wax moth" larvae that hatch, tunnel through, and destroy comb that contains bee larvae and their honey stores. The tunnels they create are lined with silk, which entangles and starves emerging bees. Destruction of honeycombs also results in honey leaking and being wasted. A healthy hive can manage wax moths, but weak colonies, unoccupied hives, and stored frames can be decimated.

Small hive beetle (Aethina tumida) is native to Africa but has now spread to most continents. It is a serious pest among honey bees unadapted to it.

Varroa destructor, the Varroa mite, is an established pest of two species of honey bee through many parts of the world, and is blamed by many researchers as a leading cause of CCD.

Acarapis woodi, the tracheal mite, infests the trachea of honey bees.

PREDATORS

Most predators prefer not to eat honeybees due to their unpleasant sting, but they still have some predators. These include large animals such as skunks or bears, which are after the honey and brood in the nest as well as the adult bees themselves. Some birds will also eat bees (for example, bee-eaters, which are named for their bee-centric diet), as do some robber flies, such as Mallophora ruficauda, which is a pest of apiculture in South America due to its habit of eating workers while they are foraging in meadows

According to U.N. FAO data, the world's beehive stock rose from around 50 million in 1961 to around 83 million in 2014, which comes to about 1.3% average annual growth. Average annual growth has accelerated to 1.9% since 2009.

THE SECRETS OF BEEKEEPING

CHALLENGING TIMES FOR BEEKEEPERS AND BEES

Unlike pets, bees have a very cyclical life cycle and beekeepers have to work tirelessly to provide the bees what they need to keep them alive. Currently, bees throughout the world are facing unprecedented extension rates, and according to Holmes, one of the reasons is a very dire lack of forage in our environment, which has a direct impact on bee nutrition.

Holmes says that currently, in Florida, there is much less forage than a couple of decades ago. For instance, one of the most delicious honey produced in Florida is Gallberry Honey. However, this type of honey is rare and not easy to get anymore. Holmes explains that the pine trees that grow among the gallberry bushes are sought for their pine needles. Unfortunately, chemical treatment is used on the ground to deter from anything else growing on the forest floor.

Another type of very popular honey produced on the East Coast of the United States is Orange blossom honey. However, the crops are suffering, and that affects the production of honey. 15 years ago, Holmes used to make 120 pounds (54 kg) of orange blossom honey per one bee colony, while today, the beekeeper makes 10 to 20 pounds (5-10 kg) of orange blossom honey per colony.

In 2018, scientists revealed alarming numbers, stating that within a winter period of 6 months, 40% of honeybee colonies in the US died. Over the past 15 years, scientists have been talking about the colony collapse disorder, which might be caused by the use of pesticides, various infections or changes in beekeeping practices.

Holmes encourages every farmer and beekeeper not to wait for governments to change the laws and regulations, but to take their own responsibility and increase the diversity of the food they grow, reduce the use of chemicals, and plant as many pollinator-friendly plants as possible.

SAFETY GEAR

For anyone who might consider keeping the bees and so in this way to help to increase pollination, Holmes stresses the importance of having a proper safety gear. She advises while working with the bees to wear light and loose clothes as bees do not like dark colors. A long sleeve shirt or a bee jacket, which is designed to protect from stinging, are also part of safety gear along with a hat with an attached veil and gloves.

Every beekeeper also needs to have a so-called J-hook hive tool, which has a curved hook. It is used primarily for prying the hive frames loose while reducing potential damage done to both the frame and comb. Another important equipment that beekeepers have is a smoker, which is used to calm the bees so that a beekeeper can access a hive.

If you decide to keep bees, it is important to have a hive correctly set up. Holmes notes that beekeepers need to make sure they have good access to hives and bees are up off the ground to be free from predation and flooding.

The experienced beekeeper also advises not to stand in front of a hive, where bees come and go, as every bee colony has guard bees who might come and sting you. The best way to enter the hive is from the side.

INSIDE A BEEHIVE

Homes advises to check the hives every two weeks, or weekly when there is an active nectar flow. Even though bees can fly a mile or more to get some food and water, most beekeepers make sure to put some water source near an apiary. Every time they inspect the hives, beekeepers determine the health and productivity of the colony.

One of the essential tasks of every beehive inspection is to find eggs, which indicate that the bee queen is alive and well and laying eggs. Every beekeeper also examines the brood pattern, which, if it is tight and compact, indicates a good, healthy queen.

You should place the bees in the safe area, where people and animals do not walk and do not cross bee flying paths.

Holmes adds that typically beekeepers are plant keepers too so that bees and other pollinators could pollinate the plants and survive in this way, while we, at the same time, could eat the food we like, for instance, tasty fruits or vegetables.

Currently, Slow Food advocates for the European Citizens' Initiative "Save Bees and Farmers", which aims to phase out synthetic pesticides in Europe by 2035, to restore biodiversity and help farmers in transition, and so to save bees from extinction in Europe.

HISTORY

Early history

Honey seeker depicted on 8,000-year-old cave painting near Valencia, Spain

Depictions of humans collecting honey from wild bees date to 10,000 years ago. Beekeeping in pottery vessels began about 9,000 years ago in North Africa. Domestication of bees is shown in Egyptian art from around 4,500 years ago. Simple hives and smoke were used and honey was stored in jars, some of which were found in the tombs of pharaohs such as Tutankhamun. It wasn't until the 18th century that European understanding of the colonies and biology of bees allowed the construction of the movable comb hive so that honey could be harvested without destroying the entire colony.

At some point humans began to attempt to maintain colonies of wild bees in artificial hives made from hollow logs, wooden boxes, pottery vessels, and woven straw baskets or "skeps". Traces of beeswax are found in potsherds throughout the Middle East beginning about 7000 BCE.

Honeybees were kept in Egypt from antiquity. On the walls of the sun temple of Nyuserre Ini from the Fifth Dynasty, before 2422 BCE, workers are depicted blowing smoke into hives as they are removing honeycombs. Inscriptions detailing the production of honey are found on the tomb of Pabasa from the Twenty-sixth Dynasty (c. 650 BCE), depicting pouring honey in jars and cylindrical hives. Sealed pots of honey were found in the grave goods of pharaohs such as Tutankhamun.

In prehistoric Greece (Crete and Mycenae), there existed a system of high-status apiculture, as can be concluded from the finds of hives, smoking pots, honey extractors and other beekeeping paraphernalia in Knossos. Beekeeping was considered a highly valued industry controlled by beekeeping overseers—owners of gold rings depicting apiculture scenes rather than religious ones as they have been reinterpreted recently.

Archaeological finds relating to beekeeping have been discovered at Rehov, a Bronze and Iron Age archaeological site in the Jordan Valley, Israel. Thirty intact hives, made of straw and unbaked clay, were discovered by archaeologist Amihai Mazar in the ruins of the city, dating from about 900 BCE. The hives were found in orderly rows, three high, in a manner that could have accommodated around 100 hives, held more than 1 million bees and had a potential annual yield of 500 kilograms of honey and 70 kilograms of beeswax, according to Mazar, and are evidence that an advanced honey industry existed in ancient Israel 3,000 years ago.

In ancient Greece, aspects of the lives of bees and beekeeping are discussed at length by Aristotle. Beekeeping was also documented by the Roman writers Virgil, Gaius Julius Hyginus, Varro, and Columella.

Beekeeping has also been practiced in ancient China since antiquity. In the book "Golden Rules of Business Success" written by Fan Li (or Tao Zhu Gong) during the Spring and Autumn period there are sections describing the art of beekeeping, stressing the importance of the quality of the wooden box used and how this can affect the quality of the honey. The Chinese word for honey (蜜 mì, reconstructed Old Chinese pronunciation *mjit) was borrowed from Indo-European proto-Tocharian language, the source of "honey", from proto-Tocharian *ḿət(ə) (where *ḿ is palatalized; cf. Tocharian B mit), cognate with English mead.

The ancient Maya domesticated a separate species of stingless bee. The use of stingless bees is referred to as meliponiculture, named after bees of the tribe Meliponini —such as Melipona quadrifasciata in Brazil. This variation of bee keeping still occurs around the world today. For instance, in Australia, the stingless bee Tetragonula carbonaria is kept for production of their honey.

SCIENTIFIC STUDY OF HONEY BEES

It was not until the 18th century that European natural philosophers undertook the scientific study of bee colonies and began to understand the complex and hidden world of bee biology. Preeminent among these scientific pioneers were Swammerdam, René Antoine Ferchault de Réaumur, Charles Bonnet, and François Huber. Swammerdam and Réaumur were among the first to use a microscope and dissection to understand the internal biology of honey bees. Réaumur was among the first to construct a glass walled observation hive to better observe activities within hives. He observed queens laying eggs in open cells, but still had no idea of how a queen was fertilized; nobody had ever witnessed the mating of a queen and drone and many theories held that queens were "self-fertile," while others believed that a vapor or "miasma" emanating from the drones fertilized queens without direct physical contact. Huber was the first to prove by observation and experiment that queens are physically inseminated by drones outside the confines of hives, usually a great distance away.

Following Réaumur's design, Huber built improved glass-walled observation hives and sectional hives that could be opened like the leaves of a book. This allowed inspecting individual wax combs and greatly improved direct observation of hive activity. Although he went blind before he was twenty, Huber employed a secretary, François Burnens, to make daily observations, conduct careful experiments, and keep accurate notes over more than twenty years. Huber confirmed that a hive consists of one queen who is the mother of all the female workers and male drones in the colony. He was also the first to confirm that mating with drones takes place outside of hives and that queens are inseminated by a number of successive matings with male drones, high in the air at a great distance from their hive. Together, he and Burnens dissected bees under the microscope and were among the first to describe the ovaries and spermatheca, or sperm store, of queens as well as the penis of male drones. Huber is universally regarded as "the father of modern bee-science" and his "Nouvelles Observations sur Les Abeilles (or "New Observations on Bees") [16] revealed all the basic scientific truths for the biology and ecology of honeybees.

INVENTION OF THE MOVABLE COMB HIVE

Rural beekeeping in the 16th century

Early forms of honey collecting entailed the destruction of the entire colony when the honey was harvested. The wild hive was crudely broken into, using smoke to suppress the bees, the honeycombs were torn out and smashed up — along with the eggs, larvae and honey they contained. The liquid honey from the destroyed brood nest was strained through a sieve or basket. This was destructive and unhygienic, but for hunter-gatherer societies this did not matter, since the honey was generally consumed immediately and there were always more wild colonies to exploit. But in settled societies the destruction of the bee colony meant the loss of a valuable resource; this drawback made beekeeping both inefficient and something of a "stop and start" activity. There could be no continuity of production and no possibility of selective breeding, since each bee colony was destroyed at harvest time, along with its precious queen.

During the medieval period abbeys and monasteries were centers of beekeeping, since beeswax was highly prized for candles and fermented honey was used to make alcoholic mead in areas of Europe where vines would not grow. The 18th and 19th centuries saw successive stages of a revolution in beekeeping, which allowed the bees themselves to be preserved when taking the harvest.

Intermediate stages in the transition from the old beekeeping to the new were recorded for example by Thomas Wildman in 1768/1770, who described advances over the destructive old skep-based beekeeping so that the bees no longer had to be killed to harvest the honey. Wildman for example fixed a parallel array of wooden bars across the top of a straw hive or skep (with a separate straw top to be fixed on later) "so that there are in all seven bars of deal" [in a 10-inch-diameter (250 mm) hive] "to which the bees fix their combs". He also described using such hives in a multi-storey configuration, foreshadowing the modern use of supers: he described adding (at a proper time) successive straw hives below, and eventually removing the ones above when free of brood and filled with honey, so that the bees could be separately preserved at the harvest for a following season. Wildman also described a further development, using hives with "sliding frames" for the bees to build their comb, foreshadowing more modern uses of movable-comb hives. Wildman's book acknowledged the advances in knowledge of bees previously made by Swammerdam, Maraldi, and de Réaumur—he included a lengthy translation of Réaumur's account of the natural history of bees—and he also described the initiatives of others in designing hives for the preservation of bee-life when taking the harvest, citing in particular reports from Brittany dating from the 1750s, due to Comte de la Bourdonnaye. However, the forerunners of the modern hives with movable frames that are mainly used today are considered the traditional basket top bar (movable comb) hives of Greece, known as "Greek beehives". The oldest testimony on their use dates back to 1669 although it is probable that their use is more than 3000 years old.

The 19th century saw this revolution in beekeeping practice completed through the perfection of the movable comb hive by the American Lorenzo Lorraine Langstroth. Langstroth was the first person to make practical use of Huber's earlier discovery that there was a specific spatial measurement between the wax combs, later called the bee space, which bees do not block with wax, but keep as a free passage. Having determined this bee space (between 5 and 8 mm, or 1/4 to 3/8"), Langstroth then designed a series of wooden frames within a rectangular hive box, carefully maintaining the correct space between successive frames, and found that the bees would build parallel honeycombs in the box without bonding them to each other or to the hive walls. This enables the beekeeper to slide any frame out of the hive for inspection, without harming the bees or the comb, protecting the eggs, larvae and pupae contained within the cells. It also meant that combs containing honey could be gently removed and the honey extracted without destroying the comb. The emptied honey combs could then be returned to the bees intact for refilling. Langstroth's book, The Hive and Honey-bee, published in 1853, described his rediscovery of the bee space and the development of his patent movable comb hive.

The invention and development of the movable-comb-hive fostered the growth of commercial honey production on a large scale in both Europe and the US.

EVOLUTION OF HIVE DESIGNS

Langstroth's design for movable comb hives was seized upon by apiarists and inventors on both sides of the Atlantic and a wide range of moveable comb hives were designed and perfected in England, France, Germany and the United States. Classic designs evolved in each country: Dadant hives and Langstroth hives are still dominant in the US; in France the De-Layens trough-hive became popular and in the UK a British National hive became standard as late as the 1930s although in Scotland the smaller Smith hive is still popular. In some Scandinavian countries and in Russia the traditional trough hive persisted until late in the 20th century and is still kept in some areas. However, the Langstroth and Dadant designs remain ubiquitous in the US and also in many parts of Europe, though Sweden, Denmark, Germany, France and Italy all have their own national hive designs. Regional variations of hive evolved to reflect the climate, floral productivity and the reproductive characteristics of the various subspecies of native honey bee in each bio-region.

The differences in hive dimensions are insignificant in comparison to the common factors in all these hives: they are all square or rectangular; they all use movable wooden frames; they all consist of a floor, brood-box, honey super, crown-board and roof. Hives have traditionally been constructed of cedar, pine, or cypress wood, but in recent years hives made from injection molded dense polystyrene have become increasingly important.

Hives also use queen excluders between the brood-box and honey supers to keep the queen from laying eggs in cells next to those containing honey intended for consumption. Also, with the advent in the 20th century of mite pests, hive floors are often replaced for part of (or the whole) year with a wire mesh and removable tray.

FIXED COMB HIVES

A fixed comb hive is a hive in which the combs cannot be removed or manipulated for management or harvesting without permanently damaging the comb. Almost any hollow structure can be used for this purpose, such as a log gum, skep, wooden box, or a clay pot or tube. Fixed comb hives are no longer in common use in industrialized countries, and are illegal in places that require movable combs to inspect for problems such as varroa and American foulbrood. In many developing countries fixed comb hives are widely used and, because they can be made from any locally available material.

Beekeeping using fixed comb hives is an essential part of the livelihoods of many communities in poor countries. The charity Bees for Development recognizes that local skills to manage bees in fixed comb hives are widespread in Africa, Asia, and South America. Internal size of fixed comb hives range from 32.7 liters (2000 cubic inches) typical of the clay tube hives used in Egypt to 282 liters (17209 cubic inches) for the Perone hive. Straw skeps, bee gums, and unframed box hives are unlawful in most US states, as the comb and brood cannot be inspected for diseases. However, skeps are still used for collecting swarms by hobbyists in the UK, before moving them into standard hives. Quinby used box hives to produce so much honey that he saturated the New York market in the 1860s. His writings contain excellent advice for management of bees in fixed comb hives.

MODERN BEEKEEPING

Top bar hives have been widely adopted in Africa where they are used to keep tropical honeybee ecotypes. Their advantages include being light weight, adaptable, easy to harvest honey, and less stressful for the bees. Disadvantages include combs that are fragile and cannot usually be extracted and returned to the bees to be refilled and that they cannot easily be expanded for additional honey storage.

A growing number of amateur beekeepers are adopting various top-bar hives similar to the type commonly found in Africa. Top bar hives were originally used as a traditional beekeeping method in Greece and Vietnam with a history dating back over 2000 years. These hives have no frames and the honey-filled comb is not returned after extraction. Because of this, the production of honey is likely to be somewhat less than that of a frame and super based hive such as Langstroth or Dadant. Top bar hives are mostly kept by people who are more interested in having bees in their garden than in honey production per se. Some of the most well known top-bar hive designs are the Kenyan Top Bar Hive with sloping sides, the Tanzanian Top Bar Hive with straight sides, and Vertical Top Bar Hives, such as the Warre or "People's Hive" designed by

Abbe Warre in the mid-1900s.

The initial costs and equipment requirements are typically much less than other hive designs. Scrap wood or #2 or #3 pine can often be used to build a nice hive. Top-bar hives also offer some advantages to interacting with the bees and the amount of weight that must be lifted is greatly reduced. Top-bar hives are being widely used in developing countries in Africa and Asia as a result of the Bees for Development program. Since 2011, a growing number of beekeepers in the U.S. are using various top-bar hives.

VERTICAL STACKABLE HIVES

There are three types of vertical stackable hives: hanging or top-access frame, sliding or side-access frame, and top bar.

Hanging frame hives include Langstroth, the British National, Dadant, Layens, and Rose, differing primarily by size or number of frames. The Langstroth was the first successful top-opened hive with movable frames. Many other hive designs are based on the principle of bee space first described by Langstroth, and is a descendant of Jan Dzierzon's Polish hive designs. Langstroth hives are the most common size in the United States and much of the world; the British National is the most common size in the United Kingdom; Dadant and Modified Dadant hives are widely used in France and Italy, and Layens by some beekeepers, where their large size is an advantage. Square Dadant hives–often called 12 frame Dadant or Brother Adam hives–are used in large parts of Germany and other parts of Europe by commercial beekeepers.

Any hanging frame hive design can be built as a sliding frame design. The AZ Hive, the original sliding frame design, integrates hives using Langstroth-sized frames into a honey house so as to streamline the workflow of honey harvest by localization of labor, similar to cellular manufacturing. The honey house can be a portable trailer, allowing the beekeeper to haul the hives to a site and provide pollination services.

Top bar stackable hives simply use top bars instead of full frames. The most common type is the Warre hive, although any hive with hanging frames can be made into a top bar stackable hive by using only the top bar and not the whole frame. This may work less-well with larger frames, where crosscomb and attachment can occur more-readily.

PROTECTIVE CLOTHING

Most beekeepers also wear some protective clothing. Novice beekeepers usually wear gloves and a hooded suit or hat and veil. Experienced beekeepers sometimes elect not to use gloves because they inhibit delicate manipulations. The face and neck are the most important areas to protect, so most beekeepers wear at least a veil. Defensive bees are attracted to the breath, and a sting on the face can lead to much more pain and swelling than a sting elsewhere, while a sting on a bare hand can usually be quickly removed by fingernail scrape to reduce the amount of venom injected.

Traditionally beekeeping clothing was pale colored and this is still very common today. This is because of the natural color of cotton and cost of coloring was an expense not warranted for workwear, though some consider this is to provide better differentiation from the colony's natural predators (such as bears and skunks) which tend to be dark-colored. It is now known that bees see in ultraviolet and are also attracted to scent. So the type of fabric conditioner used has more impact than the color of the fabric.

'Stings' retained in clothing fabric continue to pump out an alarm pheromone that attracts aggressive action and further stinging attacks. Washing suits regularly, and rinsing gloved hands in vinegar minimizes attraction.

SMOKER

Smoke is the beekeeper's third line of defense. Most beekeepers use a "smoker"—a device designed to generate smoke from the incomplete combustion of various fuels. Smoke calms bees; it initiates a feeding response in anticipation of possible hive abandonment due to fire. Smoke also masks alarm pheromones released by guard bees or when bees are squashed in an inspection. The ensuing confusion creates an opportunity for the beekeeper to open the hive and work without triggering a defensive reaction. In addition, when a bee consumes honey the bee's abdomen distends, supposedly making it difficult to make the necessary flexes to sting, though this has not been tested scientifically.

Many types of fuel can be used in a smoker as long as it is natural and not contaminated with harmful substances. These fuels include hessian, twine, burlap, pine needles, corrugated cardboard, and mostly rotten or punky wood. Indian beekeepers, especially in Kerala, often use coconut fibers as they are readily available, safe, and of negligible expense. Some beekeeping supply sources also sell commercial fuels like pulped paper and compressed cotton, or even aerosol cans of smoke. Other beekeepers use sumac as fuel because it ejects lots of smoke and doesn't have an odor.

Some beekeepers are using "liquid smoke" as a safer, more

convenient alternative. It is a water-based solution that is sprayed onto the bees from a plastic spray bottle.

Torpor may also be induced by the introduction of chilled air into the hive – while chilled carbon dioxide may have harmful long-term effects.

EFFECTS OF STINGS AND OF PROTECTIVE MEASURES

Some beekeepers believe that the more stings a beekeeper receives, the less irritation each causes, and they consider it important for safety of the beekeeper to be stung a few times a season. Beekeepers have high levels of antibodies (mainly IgG) reacting to the major antigen of bee venom, phospholipase A2 (PLA). Antibodies correlate with the frequency of bee stings.

The entry of venom into the body from bee-stings may also be hindered and reduced by protective clothing that allows the wearer to remove stings and venom sacs with a simple tug on the clothing. Although the stinger is barbed, a worker bee is less likely to become lodged into clothing than human skin.

If a beekeeper is stung by a bee, there are many protective measures that should be taken in order to make sure the affected area does not become too irritated. The first cautionary step that should be taken following a bee sting is removing the stinger without squeezing the attached venom glands. A quick scrape with a fingernail is effective and intuitive. This step is effective in making sure that the venom injected does not spread, so the side effects of the sting will go away sooner. Washing the affected area with soap and water is also a good way to stop the spread of venom. The last step that needs to be taken is to apply ice or a cold compress to the stung area.

NATURAL BEEKEEPING

The natural beekeeping movement believes that bee hives are weakened by modern beekeeping and agricultural practices, such as crop spraying, hive movement, frequent hive inspections, artificial insemination of queens, routine medication, and sugar water feeding.

Related to natural beekeeping, urban beekeeping is an attempt to revert to a less industrialized way of obtaining honey by utilizing small-scale colonies that pollinate urban gardens. Urban apiculture has undergone a renaissance in the first decade of the 21st century, and urban beekeeping is seen by many as a growing trend.

Some have found that "city bees" are actually healthier than "rural bees" because there are fewer pesticides and greater biodiversity in the urban gardens. Urban bees may fail to find forage, however, and homeowners can use their landscapes to help feed local bee populations by planting flowers that provide nectar and pollen. An environment of year-round, uninterrupted bloom creates an ideal environment for colony reproduction.

CONCLUSION

Beekeeping (or apiculture) is the maintenance of bee colonies, commonly in man-made hives, by humans. Most such bees are honey bees in the genus Apis, but other honey-producing bees such as Melipona stingless bees are also kept. A beekeeper (or apiarist) keeps bees in order to collect their honey and other products that the hive produce (including beeswax, propolis, flower pollen, bee pollen, and royal jelly), to pollinate crops, or to produce bees for sale to other beekeepers. A location where bees are kept is called an apiary or "bee yard".

Made in the USA
Monee, IL
13 May 2021